THE
LONG JOURNEY
FROM SPACE

THE LONG JOURNEY FROM SPACE

by SEYMOUR SIMON

Crown Publishers, Inc.   New York

ALSO BY SEYMOUR SIMON

Animal Fact/Animal Fable
The Long View into Space
The Smallest Dinosaurs

PICTURE CREDITS

The author wishes to acknowledge for the use of photographs:
Hale Observatories: Frontispiece, 13, 14, 15, 16, 17, 18, 20, 24, 26, 29
Yerkes Observatory Photograph, University of Chicago: 6, 12, 25, 28, 30, 31, 32, 33, 34, 36, 38, 40, 41, 44, 47
NASA: 23, 27
American Museum of Natural History: 39, 42, 43 top and bottom, 46
Bettmann Archives: 9
Granger Collection: 10, 11
Eastman Kodak Company: 21
Smithsonian Institution: 45

Manufactured in the United States of America
Published simultaneously in Canada
by General Publishing Company Limited
10 9 8 7 6 5 4 3 2
The text of this book is set in 14 point Palatino.
The illustrations are black-and-white photographs.
Library of Congress Cataloging in Publication Data
Simon, Seymour.
The long journey from space.
1. Comets—Juvenile literature. 2. Meteors—Juvenile
literature.   I. Title.
QB721.5.S55   523.6   81-22038
ISBN: 0-517-54541-1   AACR2

TO JOYCE

INTRODUCTION

Once in a while a beautiful shining object appears in the night sky. It looks like a patch of misty light with a long tail. We call it a comet.

Much more common than comets are meteors. They look like streaks of light. Most last for only an instant. If you watch the night sky, you can see a few meteors every night. Some people call meteors shooting, or falling, stars. But they are not stars.

In this book we will look at comets and meteors, find out what they are and what they mean to us on planet Earth.

COMETS IN HISTORY

Comets have always made news, usually bad news. In the past, many people, because they rarely saw a comet, believed that comets were warnings of disasters. They believed that the appearance of a comet in the sky forecasted a war, a plague, an earthquake, or an important person's death.

The photograph shows a panel of the Bayeux Tapestry, a woven wall hanging made in the Middle Ages. It shows a bright comet that appeared in A.D. 1066. England was conquered by the Normans that year, and many people believed that the comet had foretold the defeat of the English.

Aristotle, a Greek philosopher who lived more than two thousand years ago, believed that comets were patches of air that somehow caught fire. The patch of burning air would move about and finally burn out and disappear.

For hundreds of years, astronomers agreed with Aristotle. They did not believe comets were heavenly bodies like the stars and planets. This old print shows one artist's idea of different kinds of comets. Some of the comets look like other objects, such as a sword.

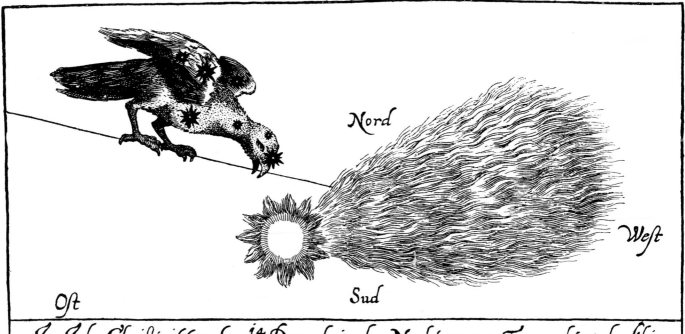

*I*t was not until the sixteenth century that Aristotle's beliefs about comets were proved wrong. In 1577 a great comet appeared in the sky and was studied by Tycho Brahe, a Danish astronomer.

Tycho wanted to find out how far away this comet was. He compared his observations with those of astronomers in Prague, who were more than four hundred miles away from him. Using mathematics, Tycho figured that the comet was at least three times farther away from Earth than the moon. That meant that the comet was a heavenly body, not a patch of burning air as Aristotle had thought.

Not everyone believed Tycho. Here is a print made one hundred years after Tycho's work. The artist shows a comet meeting a bird in midair. That would not have been possible if comets were as far away as Tycho had estimated.

At least fifteen hundred comets have been seen and recorded in the past two thousand years. This print is of a comet that appeared in 1811; it was visible for eighteen months. Its tail was more than 90 million miles long and 15 million miles wide. Some people believed it was responsible for the sweet grapes that were made into fine wines that year. Until the end of the century wine catalogues mentioned the great "comet wine" of 1811.

les conjectures du Pont Neuf, ou les effets merveilleux de la Comete vue en 1811.

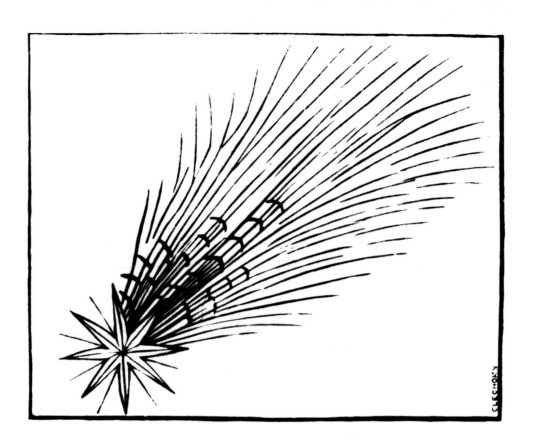

HALLEY'S COMET

In 1682 another great comet appeared in the skies. Edmund Halley, an English astronomer, carefully studied its path among the stars. Then Halley collected all the reports he could find on great comets of the past, including this drawing made by an observer of the Great Comet of 1456. He studied reports of this comet and the great comets that appeared in 1531 and 1607. The reports showed the dates the comets appeared and their paths.

*H*alley began to wonder if the comets of 1456, 1531, and 1607 were the same comet he saw in 1682. After studying the reports, Halley used mathematics to work out an orbit, or path, for the comet of 1682. His calculations showed that the comet moved through the same orbit as the earlier ones, and each appeared about every seventy-five or seventy-six years. Halley decided they must indeed be the same comet and predicted that the comet would return at Christmastime in 1758.

In the winter of 1758 astronomers all over Europe eagerly scanned the skies. On Christmas night, a German farmer using a handmade telescope spotted the comet. Halley's prediction was right, but unfortunately he died before the comet appeared. In his honor the comet was named after him.

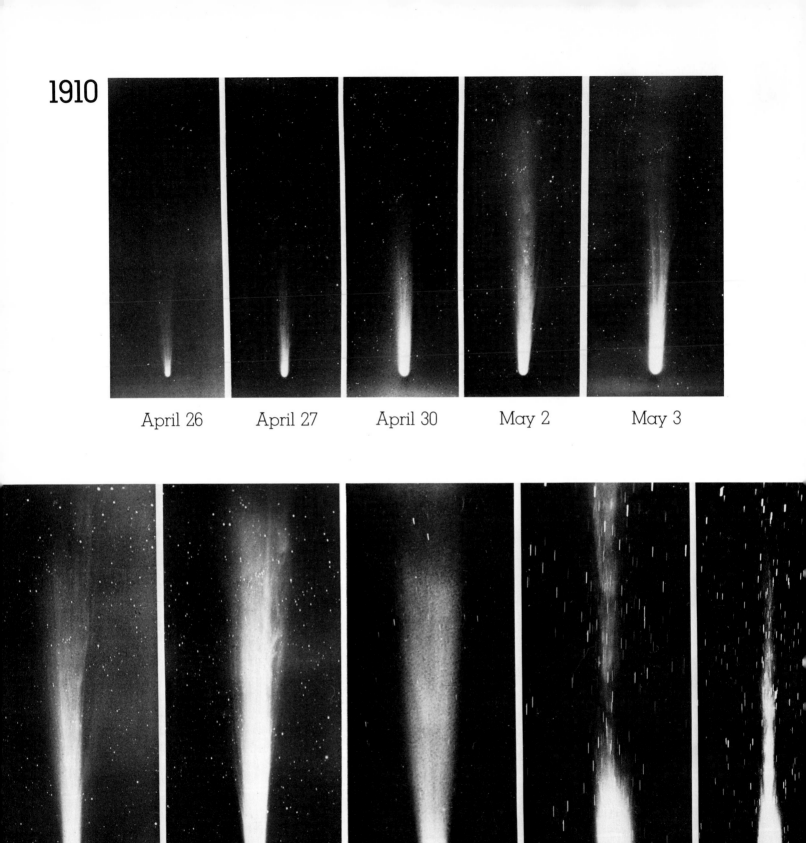

1910

April 26   April 27   April 30   May 2   May 3

May 4   May 6   May 15   May 23   May 28

When Halley's comet returned in 1910, astronomers said that Earth would pass through the comet's tail, which is made of gas. People became frightened because they thought the gas would poison them. Some people bought "anticomet" pills or bottles of oxygen. Others hid in closed rooms or in mines and caves.

Earth did pass through the comet's tail, but nothing terrible happened. How could it? A comet's tail is so thin that it is the closest thing to nothing. If all the gases in the tail were squeezed together, they could fit in a space the size of a suitcase.

Halley's comet was a beautiful sight when it appeared in 1910. The photos show the comet over a six-week period, from April 26 to June 11. At its longest, the tail stretched across one-tenth of the sky. It was 100 million miles long, greater than the distance between Earth and the sun.

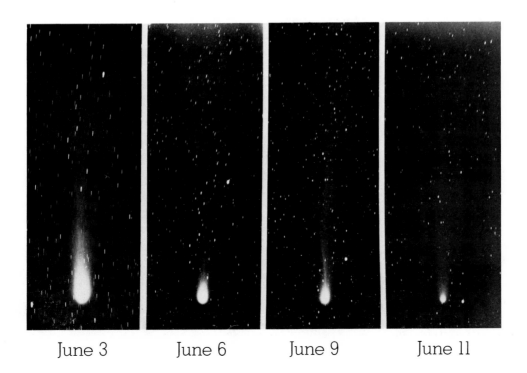

June 3　　　June 6　　　June 9　　　June 11

When Halley's comet returns in 1985, two space probes, one from Japan and one from Europe, will study the comet closely. This will be the first time that space probes will be used to study a comet. An American space probe had been designed to capture pieces of the comet, but that project has been abandoned because of a lack of money at NASA.

Observatories all around the world will study Halley's comet. They will photograph it through their telescopes and measure it with different kinds of instruments.

You will also be able to see Halley's comet if you want to. Here is the schedule.

During November 1985 you will be able to see Halley's comet only through a large telescope. By the end of December it will be visible through a small telescope or a pair of binoculars. Daily reports will tell you where to look for it in the sky.

By the third week in January 1986 you will be able to see it without a telescope or binoculars. It will be as bright as a faint star.

The comet will then pass behind the sun and will be hidden in the glare. When it comes out again, you'll be able to see it just before dawn at the end of February. By the middle of March the tail may stretch across one-sixth of the sky.

On April 11 Halley's comet will be closest to Earth. It will be very bright, but because of the angle it makes with Earth, it will be difficult to see from the United States and other countries in the Northern Hemisphere. Your best view may be around the end of April. In May the comet will be a dim object speeding away from Earth toward distant space. There is no doubt that you will also see the comet on television and in magazines and newspapers.

WHAT ARE COMETS?

*I*n the past, people knew very little about comets. We now know much more about what a comet really is. We usually cannot see a comet when it is far out in space. That's because it is only a few miles wide, too small to be seen from Earth. It is also too dark to be seen because it is covered by a layer of black dust. Underneath the black dust is a frozen ball of ice. This small dark body is the comet's *nucleus*. Some astronomers call comets dirty snowballs.

When a comet travels toward the sun, it begins to change. The pressure of light from the sun sweeps dust off the comet's surface. The dust begins to glow and forms a halo. The halo around the nucleus is called the *coma*.

As the comet comes closer to the sun, the pressure of the sunlight pushes the dust, making a glowing *tail*. This is a photograph of the Arend-Roland comet of 1957. You can see the coma and the tail. The nucleus is hidden within the coma.

1957

*H*ere are five views of the Arend-Roland comet of 1957. You can see how the coma and the tail change each day.

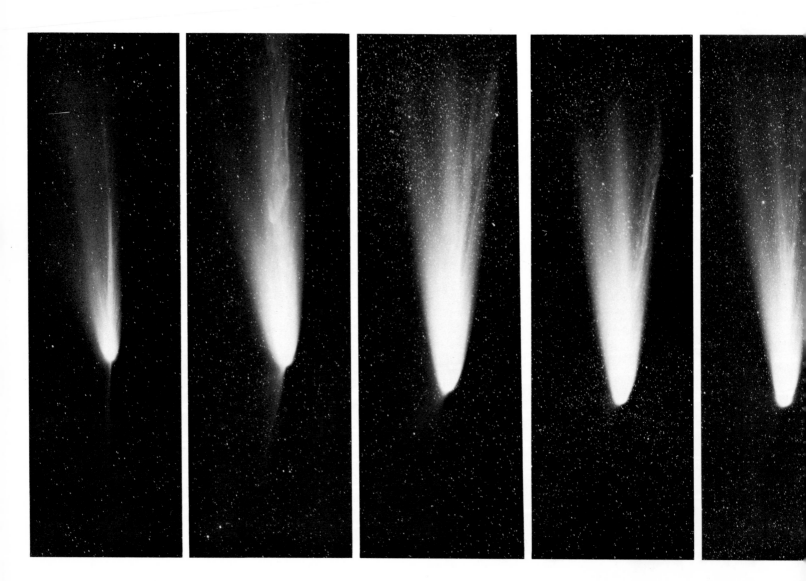

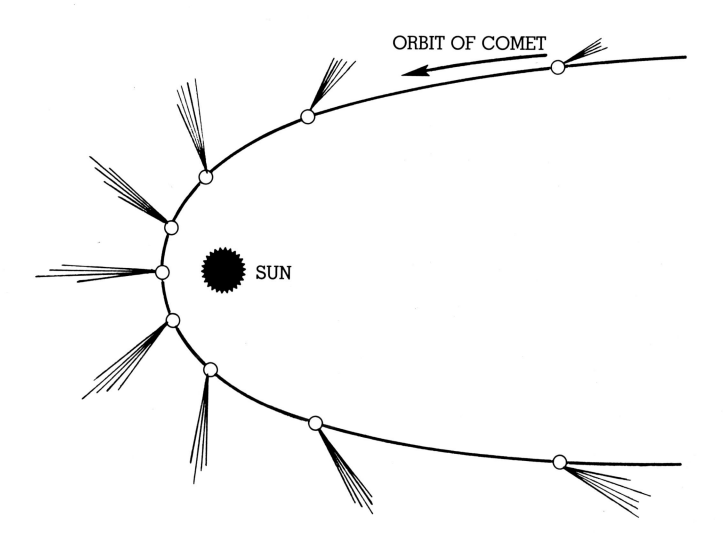

ORBIT OF COMET

SUN

A comet's tail always points away from the sun. The drawing shows what happens to the tail as a comet nears the sun and then leaves. As the comet travels away from the sun, its tail is in front of it.

*E*ncke's comet has been seen on more than fifty of its visits to the neighborhood of the sun. It comes near the sun every three and one-third years. In this photograph you can see the coma. Encke has almost no tail. The streaks are star trails that were caused by the motion of the camera as it followed the fast-moving Encke.

In November 1980 astronomers used a powerful radio beam to learn more about Encke's comet. They found that the nucleus of the comet was a solid ball about two and one-half miles wide.

*H*ere is a photograph of the comet Kohoutek taken from a satellite called *Skylab 4* on Christmas Day in 1973. The photograph was taken with a special camera by *Skylab* astronauts from above Earth's atmosphere. The large bright spots are stars. The white specks are grains in the film.

Kohoutek's tail was about 3 million miles long. Scientists found small amounts of dust, water vapor, oxygen, hydrogen, and other gases in the tail. The head of the comet was made of frozen gases, ice, and dust particles.

Kohoutek was photographed and studied more closely than any other comet in history. This photograph was taken with a large telescope from the ground on January 12, 1974. It shows the comet leaving the area of the sun. At that time the tail was about 13 million miles long. Kohoutek is now a small dark object moving quickly through the outer edges of the solar system.

Scientists learned a great deal about comets from Kohoutek, but many people were disappointed when it appeared. When Kohoutek was first discovered, it was expected to shine as brightly as the moon. Some astronomers called it the "comet of the century," but it was so dim that it could not be seen without a telescope.

*C*omet's tails are usually classified into three types. *Type I* comets have a long straight tail made of glowing gases. This is a photo of Giacobini's comet of 1906. The tail seems to be made of long strings of light.

A *Type II* comet has a broad, curving dust tail. This tail is usually longer than a Type I tail. Type I tails look bluish, whereas Type II tails look reddish. The difference in color is due to the different substances in the tails.

This is a photograph of the Ikeya-Seki comet of 1965, taken with an ordinary camera. It shows how a Type II dust tail looks to an observer without a telescope. Comet Ikeya-Seki was the first since Halley's comet in 1910 that was bright enough to be seen during the day.

*H*ere's a photo of comet West taken from a NASA rocket in 1976. Comet West's Type II dust tail measured about 50 million miles in length.

A *Type III* comet tail is rarely seen. It is sometimes called an antitail because it points away from the dust tail of the comet. The comet Arend-Roland of 1957 is a Type III comet. The photo shows a Type II tail stretching to the upper right and an antitail stretching to the lower left.

Antitails may result from sunlight reflected off dust particles that are falling toward the sun. Other kinds of Type III tails are caused by dust particles in the space around the comet.

1957

August 22

August 24

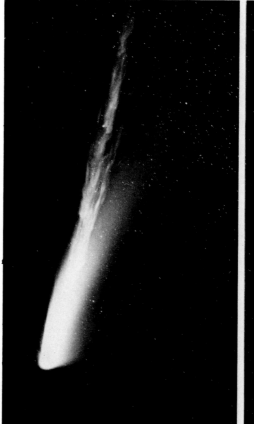

August 26

August 27

Some comets have both the straight gas tail of Type I and the curved dust tail of Type II. These are four photos of the Mrkós comet. You can see the straight gas tail to the left and the curved dust tail to the right.

Some comets have two, three, or more tails. Here is a photo of the Great Comet of 1901. You can see that it had two tails. The daylight comet of 1744 was reported to have had no less than six or seven tails.

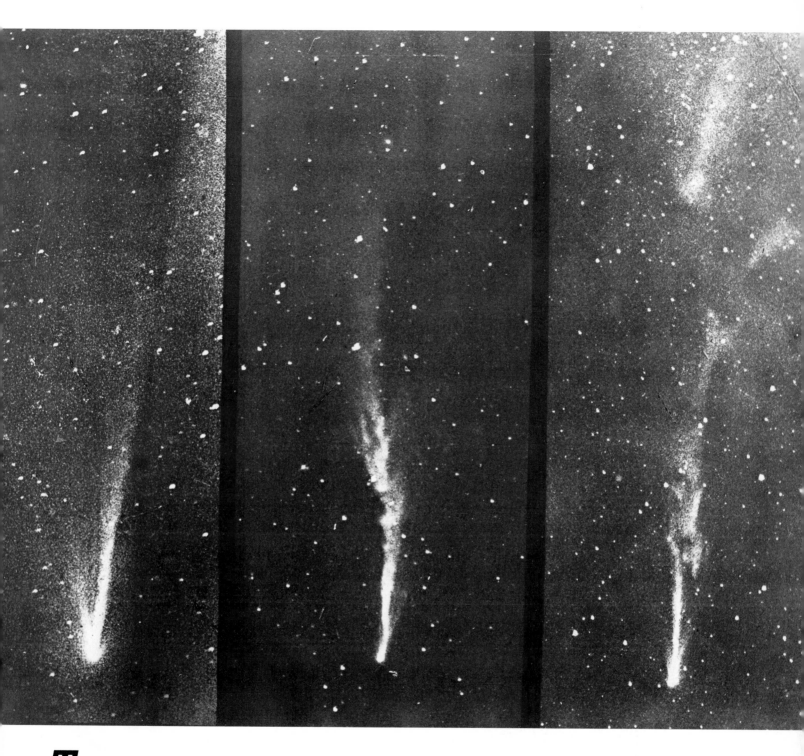

T ails may break and change very rapidly. Here are three photos, each taken one day apart, of the Brooks's comet of 1893. You can see that the tail had been shattered by the time the third photo was taken. The comet may have passed through something in space that caused the tail to break.

*E*ach year about a dozen new comets are discovered. Many are discovered by amateurs using homemade telescopes. Comets are usually named after their discoverers. A comet is also labeled with the year of its discovery and a Roman numeral.

For example, this is a photo of a comet called 1907 IV. That means that it was the fourth comet to pass near the sun in 1907. The comet is also called Daniel's comet, after its discoverer.

About once a year a comet becomes bright enough to be seen in the night sky without a telescope. Here is how Daniel's comet looked among the clouds one night. The small white specks are stars.

*S*ome comets come close to the sun and then travel far out into space, beyond the orbit of Pluto. They may not return for thousands of years or they may never return. Kohoutek's comet is one of these.

Other comets approach the sun and then travel out as far as Neptune's orbit. They may return in eighty years or so. Halley's comet is one of these.

Still other comets travel near the sun every dozen years or so. They are called short-period comets. They travel out as far as the orbit of Jupiter.

This is a photograph of a short-period comet called Brooks's comet. Brooks is a member of Jupiter's family of comets. These are comets whose paths have been changed by Jupiter's pull of gravity. Jupiter has at least fifty comets in its "family."

METEORS

*I*f you watch the sky on a clear night, you are far more likely to see a meteor than a comet. A meteor looks like a bright streak of light flashing across the sky. Some people call it a shooting star, but it is not a star.

The stars are far beyond the solar system. Like comets, meteoroids are pieces of metal or rock that travel around the sun in orbits. We cannot see most of them because they are too small.

Sometimes meteoroids speed into the atmosphere around Earth. Then the pieces become red hot and begin to glow. They are then called meteors. We see the bright flash for only a few seconds. The streak in this photograph is the trail of a meteor that is burning up in the air.

*H*ere is another photograph of a meteor trail in the night sky. To the left and above the meteor trail is the bright star Rigel in the constellation of Orion. The fuzzy patch of light in the center is the Great Nebula in Orion.

The meteor trail is millions and millions of times closer to Earth than anything else in the photograph. Spaceships sometimes collect meteor dust in Earth's atmosphere. But no spaceship from Earth has reached even the closest star.

*N*ow and then a meteor may be brighter than the brightest star. These very bright meteors are called fireballs or bolides. Fireballs often leave a trail of glowing gases that last for several minutes. Here is a photograph of a fireball. To the left of the fireball's trail is a galaxy that is made up of millions of stars.

*H*ere's a way you can show why meteors get so hot. Rub your hands against each other slowly. Now rub your hands against each other as quickly as you can. You can feel how your hands become hotter the faster you rub.

Meteoroids out in space travel very rapidly. They travel faster than a bullet shot from a gun. But there is no air for them to rub against in space. When the meteoroids come near Earth, they begin to rub against the gases that make up our planet's atmosphere. They become hot enough to glow and burn.

You can see some meteors on any clear night. Make yourself comfortable and look at the sky. You should see about six to ten meteors an hour on the average. A full moon, bright lights, or hazy skies will reduce the number you can see.

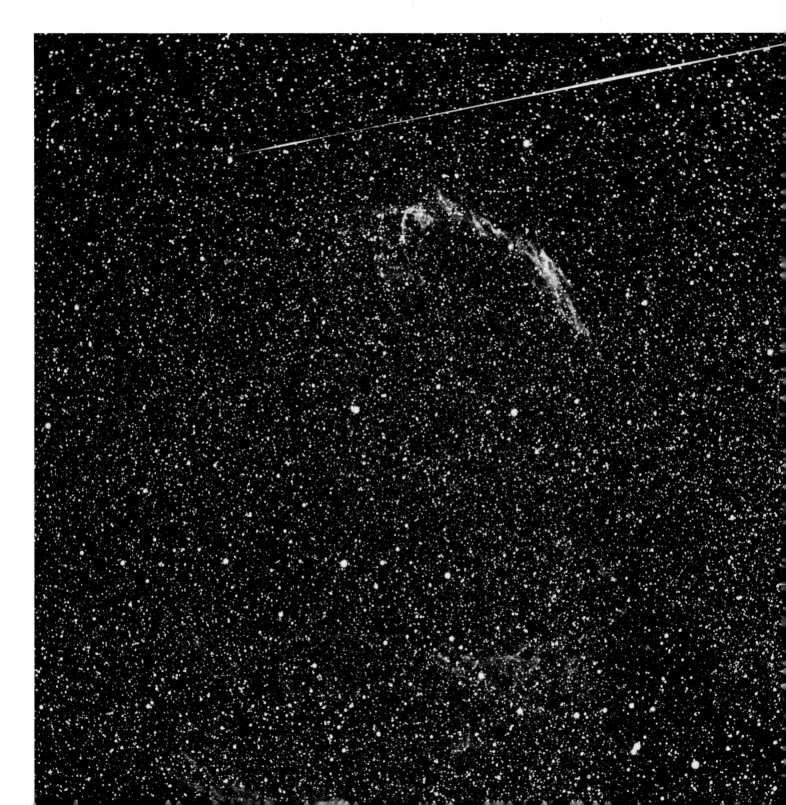

On certain nights during the year you can see more than ten meteors per hour. This is called a meteor shower, and it occurs when Earth passes through the remains of a comet.

Some meteor showers take place the same time every year. For example, about the middle of November a meteor shower looks as if it is coming from the direction of the constellation Leo. This meteor shower is called the Leonids. On the night of the Leonids, you may be able to see fifteen or twenty meteors per hour.

This is one artist's idea of a meteor shower that happened on November 13, 1833. The artist used a great deal of imagination, for it is unlikely that so many meteors fell at one time.

Here are two more drawings of meteor showers. The first is of a meteor shower of November 1868. The second is of a meteor shower of November 1872. The second drawing is much more accurate than the first one.

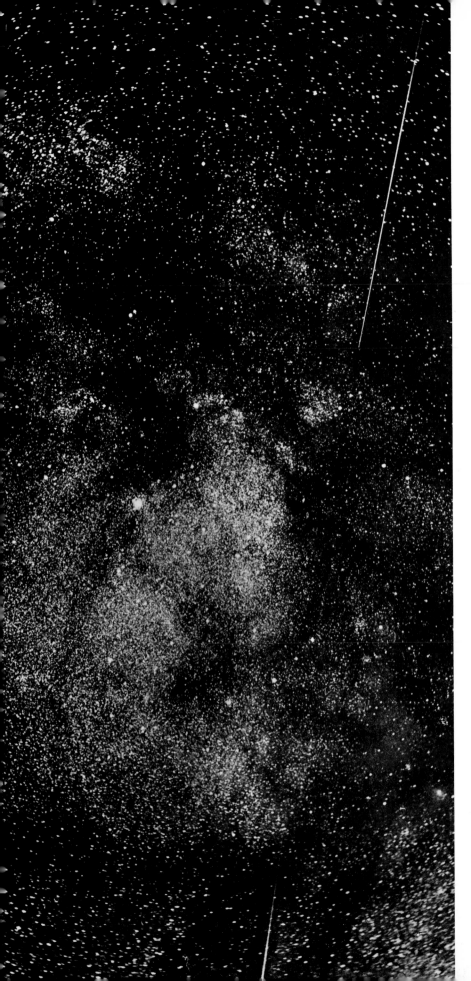

*M*ost meteors begin to heat up and glow fifty to eighty miles above Earth's surface. Fast meteors burn up sooner than slower ones. Some slow meteors continue to glow to within twenty-five miles of the surface.

A great many meteoroids enter Earth's atmosphere each day, perhaps as many as 100 million. Most of these are just tiny particles of rock. A meteoroid only one inch across may produce a fireball as bright as the moon. The two meteor trails shown in this photograph were probably produced by meteoroids that weighed less than one-hundredth of an ounce.

*I*f a meteor is very large, it may not burn up in Earth's atmosphere. It may become a brilliant fireball and then fall to Earth's surface. A meteor that reaches Earth's surface is called a *meteorite*.

More than three thousand meteorites have been collected and examined by scientists. Most are just a few inches across, such as this one, which fell in Arizona.

Many meteorites are believed to have come from the asteroid belt. The belt is a band of boulders and rocks that orbits the sun about 200 to 300 million miles out, between the orbits of Mars and Jupiter. Very small meteorites, about the size of dust specks, are believed to have come from comets.

What are your chances of being hit by a meteorite? Not very great, say scientists. One estimate is that there is a chance of one person being hit every 9,300 years.

The only case on record happened in Alabama in 1954. A woman was resting in her house when a small meteorite broke through the roof of her house, bounced off a table, and hit her in the leg. She was shocked but only slightly bruised.

*T*his is a photograph of the thirty-one-ton Ahnighito meteorite. The meteorite fell thousands of years ago in Greenland. It was brought to the American Museum of Natural History in New York City in 1906. In 1980 the Ahnighito was placed in the new Arthur Ross Meteorite Hall in the museum's Hayden Planetarium. The Ahnighito is the heaviest meteorite on display in any museum in the world.

Meteorites are classed into three main types: stony meteorites, iron meteorites, and stony-irons. Only about one in twenty of all known meteorites is iron. An even smaller number are stony-irons.

Because metal doesn't break up as easily as stone, iron meteorites can be very large. The biggest meteorite ever found was an iron one called Hoba. The Hoba meteorite weighs more than sixty tons and still lies where it fell in Namibia, Africa.

Very large meteorites weighing more than one thousand tons sometimes strike Earth. These monster rocks aren't slowed down by Earth's atmosphere. When they hit the ground, they can explode with the force of an atom bomb.

This is a photograph of the largest known meteor crater on Earth. It is in Canyon Diablo in Arizona. The crater is nearly a mile across and more than six hundred feet deep. Scientists think it was made twenty thousand years ago by a meteorite weighing 300 thousand tons.

If a meteorite of that size fell near a city today, it would cause many deaths and much damage. A recent movie called *Meteor* showed the disaster that might occur if that were to happen. But it is very unlikely. One scientist thinks that a meteorite that large could hit Earth only once in 250 thousand years.

Some scientists say that even larger meteorites have hit Earth. Such a giant meteorite hitting Earth 65 million years ago may have caused the dinosaurs to die out.

These scientists believe that a three-mile-wide meteorite struck Earth and exploded, forming an enormous cloud of dust. The dust blocked much of the sunlight for several years, causing many plants to stop growing and die. The plant-eating dinosaurs and other animals of the time died from lack of food. Then the meat-eating dinosaurs died from lack of food. This theory is still being investigated.

Comets and meteors are more than just odd-looking lights in the sky. One scientist called them "crumbs and scraps left over from the formation of the solar system."

A few years ago, scientists were able to date the age of a large meteorite that fell near the Allende Valley in Mexico. They found that the Allende meteorite was 4.6 *billion* years old. The meteorite was the oldest solid object ever touched by humans. The meteorite has helped us to tell the age of the solar system and of our planet Earth.

No one knows for sure what new things we will learn from our studies of comets and meteorites. But the search for new knowledge will continue as long as we keep our sense of wonder about the universe.